Intrusive Beauty

D0166571

The Hollis Summers Poetry Prize

GENERAL EDITOR: DAVID SANDERS

Named after the distinguished poet who taught for many years at Ohio University and made Athens, Ohio, the subject of many of his poems, this competition invites writers to submit unpublished collections of original poems. The competition is open to poets who have not published a book-length collection as well as to those who have.

Full and updated information is available on the Hollis Summers Poetry Prize web page: ohioswallow.com/poetry_prize

Intrusive Beauty

Poems

Joseph J. Capista

OHIO UNIVERSITY PRESS

ATHENS

Ohio University Press, Athens, Ohio 45701
ohioswallow.com
© 2019 by Joseph J. Capista
All rights reserved

Printed in the United States of America
Ohio University Press books are printed on acid-free paper ⊚ ™

29 28 27 26 25 24 23 22 21 20 19   5 4 3 2 1

Library of Congress Cataloging-in-Publication Data
Names: Capista, Joseph J., author.
Title: Intrusive beauty : poems / Joseph J. Capista.
Description: Athens, Ohio : Ohio University Press, 2019. | Series:
Hollis
  Summers poetry prize
Identifiers: LCCN 2018056336| ISBN 9780821423769 (paperback) |
ISBN 9780821446652 (pdf)
Subjects: | BISAC: POETRY / General.
Classification: LCC PS3603.A65 A6 2019 | DDC 811/.6--dc23
LC record available at https://lccn.loc.gov/2018056336

O, Shannon

Contents

∾

Intrusive Beauty

Telescope

Just look: the egret's white
Reflects so like a cloud

Pursuing other clouds,
Which blow just like the white

Of wind-borne sand that winds
As if it were the wave

Atumble, breaking crest
All fracture like those shells

That fall from gulls whose beaks
Resemble oyster knives,

More dull than razor clams
And drabber than the speck

Of freighter farther out
Than one might ever hope

To swim, especially you
Who sees through glass egress

So clearly now what's not
Before your eyes. But look.

Thaw

All afternoon police unearth
the dead from roadside drifts of snow.
It happens like this every spring:
a passing motorist reports
dark tint inside a melting pile
or catches sunlight glinting off
a well-sewn button or a shoe.
Perhaps a hand, a bud unbloomed,
extends there toward imagined help.
Found are those whose orbit slipped
some imperceptible degree
before we ever thought them lost.
We watched a drifter stagger through
three lanes of traffic, arms asway
as if conducting some rush hour
motet his ears alone could hear.
He waved. I almost waved right back.
In lilac light the cruisers flashed
against the dusk. Someone dug.
Someone else rerouted cars.
We drove directly home to lie
together side by side, converse
about these newly exhumed dead.
You fear, I know, our daughter woke
mid-fight to hear about our own
dissolving dreams, this falling out of,
into love. The dead are neutral ground
and so, exhausted, spent, to them
we steer our words. It's almost prayer.
Tonight they'll rise from deep inside

of me as, half-asleep, I turn
and slip my hand in yours. But first,
so that my touch won't startle you,
won't wake you from unquiet dreams,
I'll hold my hand out to the night
and let it grow a little cold.

A *Child Bird-Scarer*

After an illustration in Life in Victorian England

I started at six with tin and a stick
scattering creatures from sharp seed sown
in Shalbourne furrows. Stones moved
what clamor couldn't—starlings, crows,
a clattering of jackdaws rose
to perch on dormer sills and startle
their own glass-bent reflections, escape
a joke at which they alone cackled.
My boy, master chastened, *mind
those beasts—see that seed takes.*
So I lurked fencerows and puddles,
frightening what I knew would fly.
Sometimes a cruelty rose in me
I could not tell apart from all
I pitched at them. The stick I clutched
has doubled now in length, the tin
turned tines. Haymaking days, I wade
knee-deep in crop to stook, then bale.
I'll steal away tonight and lie
atop the brittle piles, watch stars
as small as seeds I'd sown myself.
What I remember best is chasing
a field full of black wings knowing
they would only lift, loll, and drift
one hill over, far enough they might
forget whatever it is they feared.

Weep, You Prophets, in the Shadow of Heaven

Night. Prayer. The city is dangerous again.
Sounds rise skyward in countless concentricities.
Think them inverted bells yoked

To some geography of lines. Municipality.
Think them the sound of turning earth.
I unfold the map across the tabletop, take care

To feel the rise of crease beneath my palm.
First I touch those spots I've been,
Then touch the spots I'll never be.

The largest bell ever made,
The Great Bell of Dhammazedi,
is lost at the bottom of a river.

History of the Inevitable

Fire wants to be ash, which wants
a bucket to hold it with unseeping certainty.

The bucket wants to look like the moon,
which it does some nights, while the moon

wants to be the storefront window, full
of something. But the window's coats

are tired of town's dull hooks and long
to be pitchforks, which long to be trees.

The trees envy the slow-moving cow
beneath their boughs, and the cow wants

an engine to propel it though the sharp
fence where the man rests, wondering

how he will ever go to his desire when
the universe so needs his tending hand.

Domestic Intelligence

Best trash this tulip spray
    lest, come A.M., drooped
        blossoms drop,

lest tabletop become
    again some variegated
        scattergram

impelling you to measure,
    plot those points *chance*
        and *beauty* intersect,

lest gorgeous red-gold
    nonchalance grace
        faience eggcups,

patinaed grapefruit spoons
    you set while upstairs
        wife and daughters slept,

lest over salmon crème fraîche
    and warm pear tarte tatin,
        your mind threads petals

back to florets, transfixed
    all day by what remains
        detached yet correlates.

Best nix this vase entirely.
    Avert. Preclude. Forestall.
        Best obviate astonishment

at each blossom's way
of falling into just-the-place.
As if you'll ever understand.

The Beautiful Things of the Earth Become More Dear as They Elude Pursuit

Another wave rolls over me before
I clear its crest. I haven't surfed since June.
Foam lifts me, holds me, sings me back toward shore.

Sunrise grows a little smaller, further
away. I'm sheathed in leaky neoprene.
Another wave rolls over me before

I catch, then lose, my breath: the atmosphere
and sea gleam mica, glint their pinks and greens.
Foam lifts me, holds me, sings me back toward shore

as something flickers in a distant trough;
lit windblown water droplets—jewels—they shine.
Another wave rolls over me. Before

my eyes, a distant skimmer nears and spears
a silverside. It's gorgeous, then it's gone.
Foam lifts me, holds me, sings me back toward shore.

"Your poem," said Danny, "needs more beauty. *More.*"
I paddle, touch the water to touch sun.
Another wave rolls over me before
I'm lifted, held, I'm sung right back to shore.

Exit Wound

John, 1969–1995

Your knees that afternoon were caked with dust
and other matter—life's particulate
remains unstuck from his apartment floor.
We spent three hours searching for the place.
And when your finger found the dimple just
beneath the sill (it ricocheted) I watched
your face, all day a tangled knot of pain,
grow slack. The face I saw was his, or his
age nine at Gettysburg beside the storm-
felled tree from which he yanked a musket ball.
He bit the slug like on TV and broke
his tooth. He cried. He was a boy. We knelt
a moment, touched the bullet, touched what now
tears headlong through our lives. He was a boy.

Thirtysomething Blues

Shannon

It's not the risk we mind, but consequence.
To do without at twenty-two was "in."
Yet now we've had, to have not stings. We wince

at what, in younger days, we sought: the chance
of sloughing all we never meant to own.
It's not the risk we mind, but consequence.

The job, car loan, the mortgage on the house:
the things we need are *things*, not dreams but *plans*.
How once we've had, to have not stings. We wince

at possibility should it yield less,
no lamb and cherries, nightly glass of wine.
It's not the risk, mind you, it's consequence.

We'll quit! We'll walk! We'll move to France!
Responsible adults know my refrain:
Yes, once you've had, to have not stings. I wince

mid-concert when you say, "I'll sing like this
someday." Those notes won't pay the taxman, Shan.
It's not the risks we mind, but consequences,
as once we've had—we wince—to have not stings.

SOWEBO

Southwest Baltimore

By the time the boy's tooth chips and bloody
hair mats his scalp cradled beside the spokes,
which spin and clack, this does not matter.
Not the curbside assault, not the battery.
What matters here is the grace with which
Angelo extends his hand *I like your bike*
then yanks the boy mid-wheelie, plucks him
by the collar, then bounces him down Hollins
Market's marble antebellum steps *give it to me*.
Sure, the pack moves over him like water over
a stone, holds and obscures him, their blows
a tide fists cannot fight. On the fire escape
I look away from this, notice paint flecks
dropping like they know they're lead or bags
snagged in tree limbs filling with their threats
of flight. I want to shuck the boy from the thin
shell of my closed eyelids. Some stall keeper
swings her push broom, hollers at the pack
to go on home, voice a stroller ramming a wall.
Angelo says he'll be back again later. He will.
His story is the story of every port city gone dry.
These rooftops smell of tar and mops stained
gray as alleyway bones children practice breaking.
Come dark, when the woman I married returns,
we'll swear we hear bricks working themselves
loose from bad mortar, but it's only a pot scraped
with a lucky nickel in our stairwell or the tock
of dominos on the hood of the stock-still Ford
or dreams condensing on a cracked ceiling
then falling toward those who sleep beneath.

I'll say I didn't watch the boy as he staggered
to a primer-coated station wagon, unsure exactly
what he'd learned. I know something about grace
is cruel. When I shut my eyes to forget all this
I still see the hand's motion—bright palm's arch
and strike, those fingers closing around the boy
easy as a breaking wave—clutch so smooth
and brutal I can't tell if it's born from practice
or is simply born into this world, certain it holds
something it must never, for the life of it, release.

Entreaty

Having seen the osprey
grasp then set its fish
so that en route from sea
to bay prey's eyes face
only west,
        having seen,
half-sunblind, that glint writhe
then rise to unimagined
heights on nothing but
thin air, one ultimate
kindness before spicule,
tooth, and tongue,
           having seen
struggle slacken to repose
as descending on the nest
catch glimpses the caught,
compendium of spine
and gill and jaw agape,
kaleidoscopic shambles
shimmering in scales,
             I say,
raise me like that, unmaker,
wide-eyed and broken-backed,
if only so that I, unmade,
might see for once beyond
all doubt those unknown,
unfathomable parts
that are and are not me.

Faces of Death

We waited for the latch to click,
then someone's purloined mondo film
flickered on the TV screen.
Billowed clouds of dust occluded
the skydiver whose parachute
refused to bloom as laughter rose
above the words of Dr. Gröss
whose voice-overs—clinical,
composed—prefaced each disaster,
segued napalm, village stoning,
slo-mo plunge of turbaned head,
and then dispelled with quips about
abiding laws of gravity
the tedium we felt in watching
a future suicide, ledge-shy,
surmount her waning fear of heights.
One kid barfed, one peed his pants.
I didn't flinch or sob at what
I knew was more taboo than porn,
that other miracle-in-progress.
Catechesis proclaimed death
our immortal soul's release.
As altar boys, we played along
come Sunday's scripted sacrifice,
witnessed christening and wedding,
noticed how the catafalque
held each casket off the ground
as if, by way of simple frame,
body and spirit might hang
in sacred equilibrium

as each assumed its final rest.
Yes, we knew this story's end.
Our faces blue in basement light,
we watched a man fall from the sky
then turn to dust. And then we hit
rewind and watched him rise again.

40

Dawn. Again I piss into the empty coffeepot.
Of life and of lives I have, for hours, read by lamplight.
How much of this day I know already. Overnight it rained.

I know because I awoke. Storm static on the skylight.
I know too our sycamore has begun shedding its bark.
I know children will wear this bark as armlets

as they did last year when it shed and resembled,
too, raw cinnamon. And I know the distant Angelus
rang as it did yesterday, as it will ring tomorrow

and thereafter, though I don't know whether this morning
I heard it. Because I did so yesterday and the day before,
because I take, always, more than I return, I can stare

from this window as I piss. Visible: another green world,
a sun's exquisite execution of itself across earth.
If I descend the attic stairs, I suddenly become a father.

Mid-Flight, Mid-Ascension Virgin Photograph

The mid-flight photograph reveals
the Virgin. Outside the plane is night.
A cabin window frames the frame

where, centered, stands impossibly
the Virgin, hands raised heavenward
to guide the eye, frame the blessed face.

A cloud obscures the Virgin's face.
A cloud can solve a lot of problems.
Imagine there your face, the teacher

says. We try. But it's a problem:
the Virgin's purely brushwork—
sfumato tones applied that we

might see beyond her to beyond—
and we, pure flesh. Yet the daughter
of this picture's taker can and says

the face in her mind's eye is hers.
We learn that year the eye too is
a window, just as this photograph's

another window to the Virgin.
Great revolutions in the arts, I'd later
read, are merely shifts in context.

This thought can make the photograph
a modern miracle. Decades later,
when I see the picture taker's daughter,

she looks like me—kids in tow,
tired behind her grocery cart. Her face,
her face as I write this grows hazy

the way in the mind particulars do.
It's true. Close your eyes. Along
thought's periphery, see how black

hair frames her medal of the Virgin,
how her silver V of chain leads
your eye, directs your gaze: imagine

anybody's face suspended there.
As you pursue the image's
particulars—arch of brow, a lip's

attendant curve—see each feature
held so steadily within the mind.
Now see the way each disappears.

Cornicello

I bought it at a 9th Street corner shop
to dangle from your rearview mirror where
you'd see it glimmer just beyond your eye,
part talisman, part kitsch. I hoped the hope
of every lover: that, if death should trace
his fingertip along your high-boned cheek,
this tiny, golden horn would help you cheat
his gaze, illuminate another's face.
Of course I hoped you'd pass each day unharmed.
Of course I hoped it might help us conceive.
Of course the accident still happened, love.
Of course we lost the baby. Life's uncharmed.
It hangs between us now like all unsaid
because it didn't work, because it did.

Guide to the Monumental City

Baltimore

i.

Wax applied
to *kouri* posed
outside the BMA
assumes the shape
of statuary copied
from the Greeks.

ii.

What care these flies,
drunk again on fetid
Callery pear limbs,
too close to notice
each wing's indistinct
from those thousand
trembling blossoms?

iii.

Pink-dicked,
the pit mounts
a mottled mate
chained alike
to the storefront
church stoop.

iv.

Porch steps need
painting again,
front beds tending.

So much undone
and summer unfurling
resembles only itself
unfurled —*July, July,*

I hum to the child,
smell in the air
the bay's decay.

Either I have betrayed
the world or it, me.

v.

No gods, no ecstasy.

I go inside myself
to go outside myself.

I believe in temples.

That slippage between
the universe inside
one's head and the universe
outside is called one's life.

Art's a plinth for memory.

vi.

Huzzah, Mr. Vanitas,
see what morning
light makes plain:
oyster shell that once
housed opalescence
now alley's concrete
aggregate, housing
only autumn rain.

vii.

In the driveway
of our block's
newly condemned
house, one crushed
starling whose sheen
you took yesterday
for a small pool
of oil.
     How unlikely,
you thought, a beak
afloat in a pool of oil.

viii.

These Wedgewood walls
make greener our blue spruce.
Blue whitens snow outside.
The year heaves its ho,

ho-hum atmospheres.
The larder knows its name.
Firelight, ours. The lightest stars
are those the eye won't see.

ix.

Curbside safety
glass, so smithereened,
articulates the logic
of our cosmos
scattered there before
the antipigeon strip
affixed above
the temple door.

Lost Children

Coney Island, June 9, 1941

In Weegee's photograph we see the boy
unmothered underneath the boardwalk sign,
but it's the man, his smile, on whom we fix
our gaze, white shirt, white belt, white captain's hat:
our eye holds him a beat, then wanders toward
the littoral awash with roustabouts
and idlers, women half-undressed who laugh
a little loud because lost's almost found.
But what about the boy who clings against
and to the man, child eyes forever closed?
Our object's subject blurs. We look from boy
to man to boy before it clicks: *We're him.*
Words focused, too, prove accurate, untrue:
by *we* it's *I* we mean; by *him* it's *them.*

Devotional of Daily Apprehension

When at dawn I set forth to find the bell resounding
through unclouded air I find myself beside the tide pool
of anemones, exquisite predators enamored of a world.

When at dawn I set forth to find the bell resounding
I find myself on the median strip between lanes between
cities between modes of existence dictated by geography.

When at dawn I set forth to find the bell all the cameras
break and we do the best with what we have we splice
we elide we assemble we project we call it language.

When at dawn I set forth to find the bell resounding
through unclouded air I think eight times of the bell
Satie heard imprisoned eight days for insulting a critic.

When at dawn I set forth to find the bell resounding
I imagine sometimes the bell an impossible tongued
symmetry suspended over vast fields of nitrogen.

When at dawn I set forth to find the bell resounding
through unclouded air I find myself among financial
transactions the size of microorganisms and when

viewed through the appropriate instrument no less
beautiful than these microorganisms but I am shouting
at customers that the first search engine is the poem.

When at dawn I set forth to find the bell resounding
it is my sin which is not living the world and my
solace which is *Kid A* on repeat and Russell Edson.

When at dawn I set forth to find the bell resounding
impossible meadow impossible finch impossible thistle
impossible cordgrass coneflower impossible impossible.

When at dawn I set forth to find the bell resounding
through unclouded air I worry about what others might
perceive as my growing incapacity to love the world.

When at dawn I set forth to find the bell resounding there
is never enough time and my god my children actually
need me one is cooing now and this perpetually implodes.

When I set forth to find the bell the placard reads *You are
invited to pass through this artwork. Felix Gonzales-Torres
"Untitled" (Water) 1995. Plastic beads, string, and metal.*

When at dawn I set forth to find the bell resounding
I am holding a hymnal, that facilitator of praise
and judgment and score only to one's public death.

When at dawn I set forth to find the bell resounding
a transformer thrums without relent and this sky's grid
of wire creates positive space by framing negative space.

When at dawn I set forth to find the bell resounding
I am holding the hand of my friend made unrecognizable
by an idiopathic degenerative disorder of the central

nervous system and who loves dancing and who will
die that day as I converse with the famous figure skater
about how ice is the story not the dance not the body.

When at dawn I set forth and hear the bell resounding
through unclouded air what is incandescent wound
but sky and dressing but cloud tourniquet but tongue?

When at dawn I set forth to find the bell resounding
I come to on the dune and if to bend's to ache O
these swallows how they ache supreme in flight.

In the Event of a Fire

All of them. Broken-bottle kids from Butte,
Ravalli sons of off-grid gunrunners,
daughters left to freeze just east of Kalispell
post-meth-lab mobile home explosion:
as P.O.'s slogged through intake paperwork,
I sat our fledgling charges down to view
the shelter fire-safety video,
then sign and date the corresponding form.
Montana state requirement. They heard
debrided nonfatalities compare
the smoke in slumbered lungs to pepper spray,
intone in voices à la Bronx that they
had thought someone roach-bombed their noses.
How children fidgeted as these folks spoke
of losing everything—Lladró figurines,
siblings, smooth symmetric contours of a face—
erased while they lay dreaming. New kids,
at first, were cupcakes. Within a week,
the black-eyed ones would punch a newfound pal
when Yahtzee went awry or shy incest
survivors broke the bathroom mirror
before shower time; familiar roles,
foreseeable calamities. I'd log
and tabulate behaviors on the charts
staff therapists devised, arithmetize
each action's consequence the way I solved
those proofs from my Symbolic Logic class,
intent back then on making everything
make sense. One graveyard shift I pulled that fall,
as wildfire singed the forestland

just south of town, fumes laced our gulch's dreams.
On midnight rounds, I found the boys had cracked
a bedroom window, sneaked their smoke while staff
smoked ours and hummed transistor honky-tonk.
Against the backlit foothills I could see
the fire tower where another soul
kept watch beneath a salvaged steamship bell
that never made it back down the Missouri,
see helitacks from Canyon Ferry Lake
approach the glow and drop another load
on firebreaks the hotshot crews had cleared
in lieu of back-burning. Ash drifted through
the bedroom, delicate gray remnants
from some encroaching violence we ignored,
fell soundlessly on cigarette-scarred arms
and chokecherry cheeks. I shut the window,
drew the shade. No, they didn't even wake.

Gut-Bomb

J.M.M., 1982–2011

What separates four pounds of ground
chuck elk from four of ground chuck beef
is parsley, pepper, seasoned salt.
Source: the group home's only cookbook.
So when the warden dragged a bull
to clear the highway shoulder line
or hauled a cow, her belly warm,
some poacher left trailside for rot
he phoned me. *Game?* We'd love it. Yes.
How I remember stacking cuts,
their butcher paper pristine white,
spotlit by garage freezer light
that night a plainclothes officer
cuffed Justin and loaded him
into an unmarked Chevrolet.
I knew, of course, this was a setup
staff and law enforcement plotted
lest he throw a chair or run—
best isolate the resident
avert the perp's embarrassment
before his peers to thus ensure
a peaceable transition
between the agencies. I knew,
as well, Justin's pending charge
before he did: Chinese food
delivery stickup, shotgun loaned
by a pal's dad who thought some time
out in the woods might do him good.
Was it really unexpected?
Don't ask the rape victim who flinched

that day I called her "Justin's mother."
Before each shift, I read their files
behind the padlocked office door,
court documents and case histories,
the social worker narratives
and medication logs of children
we forgot to let be children.
I knew all I could fix was supper.
Cooking elk that year taught me
to taste fear in a kill—almost
like sorghum, although not as sweet.
By spring, I smelled fear-kills
before they even struck my skillet.
Most kids mistook the elk I served
for beef, chased it down with milk
from Deer Lodge Prison's dairy stock.
Now that, Justin announced one night
before we left the kitchen table,
that's what I call a gut-bomb burger.
He coughed, then spat out something that,
the moment it hit his plate,
sounded remarkably like buckshot.

Johnny Salmon's Father Enters the Shelter Unannounced to Repo His Adjudicated Son

Beneath me, cyclone fencing sags.
Splayed across this trout pen's lid,
I ignore the *Posted* sign that warns
Violators Prosecuted
and test how close my hand can come
to what it's not supposed to touch,
eclipse the blue-tinged autumn light
aplay against the leafless maples
this constellating school appears
to hardly miss. They rise before
my eyes a little closer now,
acclimate themselves to shade.
Farm fish, I speak, though I'm alone.
None spook. So I suppose they're used
to this, suppose each night they bid
goodbye to their private big sky
as I have bid goodbye to mine,
back East and done my year-long stint
as proxy-Jesuit, the one
I undertook that I might
discern with more acuity
an act of justice from an act
of charity. A.M.D.G.

On day three of shelter school
in walks Johnny Salmon's father,
black-braided, shirtless, filigree
of blurry rez tattoos gracing
his arms and chest. He looks confused.
Around his neck, a dreamcatcher

air freshener, an offering
of sorts so I might later say
I didn't smell that which I'm not
supposed to smell. Idling curbside,
the plateless Dodge he drove by night
from St. Ignatius, Flathead country
shadowed by the Mission Range.
Sweetass beater, one kid says.
I brace myself for head-butt, fist
or sidearm, barb of gut hook knife.
He asks only for his son.
House rules stipulate, I say,
no resident may leave our care
without the proper discharge papers.
Johnny Salmon, mid-essay, drops
his pen *Salmons are like the most
prettiest fish* walks out the door
and salmon immigrate to the sea.
That afternoon I bag and seal
whatever personal effects
of his remain so D.F.S.
can claim the load next Tuesday once
he's taken into custody —
joyriding in a stolen car
his P.O. says, too much something
coursing through his blood, then deadpans
more birthday cake in Riverside.
She sounds exhausted or amused;
it's hard to tell, just as it's hard
to tell when sky turns azure from
cerulean as it reflects
along the surface of the creek.

By now I'm screaming at the trout.
They writhe, flick droplets in my eyes.

To keep the essay Johnny wrote
would violate the shelter rules
but I did. Unfolding it
and folding it again has creased
the page so much it's hard to read,
though I care less for what it says
than for those indents Johnny's pen
has pressed into the paper's white,
my only evidence these days,
it seems, such time and place exist.
On long, long walks, I study them
and know, and never seem to know,
exactly what it is they mean.
Once I rise to leave this place
I'm not supposed to be I'll find
indented in the skin along
my ribcage, chest, perfect diamonds
marking where my weight has pushed
against what holds me like a net
above another roiling mess
I can't quite reach, unsure whether
I am caught or I am saved.

Vigilante Day Parade

Worst is seeing children cuffed
and waiting while a deputy
secures the safety belt along
the cruiser's slick backseat.
After one such incident
I haul the group home residents,
in loco parentis, downtown
to watch the Vigilante Day
Parade perpetuate our West's
beloved desperado myth.
The bank is closed, traffic's blocked.
I laugh along with them at trucks
and borrowed flatbed trailers filled
with ballot-burning outlaw thugs,
anachronistic flapper floozies
courting catcalls from their pals
as they puff bubblegum cigars,
papier-mâché cattle holdings,
and limbs with twine-hanged effigies.
Cy's mother pushes to the curb.
He doesn't seem to recognize her
although all week I've known she's back
in town, seen her sleeping under
aspens in the park, wipe clean
the crimson lipstick-petals left
on someone's half-burned cigarette.
In noontime sun, she's radiant
on meth. The crowd around her tenses;
she stammers a tune on her float-
tossed kazoo then spits on the guy

beside her. He parleys with fist.
A rookie cop (we know them all)
cuffs her to a parking meter
then radios for backup while
parents account for their children
and I account for mine—no one's
tried to bolt or fight or smoke.
But Cy ignores the scene, dives
for candy coins, a plastic badge.
He's too old for this, I think.
Behind the final marching band
trot black-hatted vigilantes,
whips and Remingtons all action,
who drive the fiends and hellcats out
for good from goldless Last Chance Gulch.
Day saved, West won, we clap and whoop
amidst this pageantry, this ruckus.
We came today expecting outlaws.
We came expecting justice.

For a Daughter

While her poems kept flowers alive in every season, Dickinson's uncommon conservatory attempted the same miracle.

—Judith Farr, *The Gardens of Emily Dickinson*

As I recite your little song
about the frost-beheaded flower,
Miss Dickinson, my daughter sleeps.
I steep a boiled baby towel,
then wrap these ice-stopped water lines
beside the basement window pane
shivered by our sycamore.
Droplets, scalding, trace my veins.
At two o'clock she'll wake to nurse.
I watched her wedge her arm between
the crib's white slats tonight as if
she couldn't help but touch the world.
In Amherst once, Miss Dickinson,
a docent scolded me because
I touched your cradle. Your dress?
Scrapped, she said, for kitchen rags.
Steam blossomed from this tepid pot,
unfurled against the joists, then left
a dew that moistens dust along
our rotted sill and clouded glass.
Outside seeps a little more inside.
In frail moments such as these,
the ones I finally talk to God
and know no matter what I say
or do, the world will always be
the cruelest example of itself,
it's really you I'm talking to.
My daughter sleeps, Miss Dickinson.

Her fontanel beats heaven's time.
I knock on copper, wait, then run
the tap, but nothing inside moves.
Now everything feels cooler. Cold.
I think of you awake at dusk,
staring blackness down from gray
to powder blue, your greenhouse duel
with death to keep each iris, daisy,
bourbon rose from winter's hand.
I see my breath. Before my daughter
wakes, Miss Dickinson, I think
of you, that moment you kindled
in your house of glass a fire.
Loved well, it bloomed.

Jellyfish

Crystal itch
adrift amid summer
swimmers,

votary
of tidal pull
and current flux,

you're such symmetric
velvet dazzle,
such quizzing glass,

such ancient
inauspicious kisser
pulsing now

these shallows,
shimmer elegance
in sea élan—

bloom rococo
blooms and swarm
deluxe swarms,

luminesce
in galaxies
as skull-swum

dreams, my tangled,
tentacled excess,
my ambient

approximate,
my appraisal
of that space

between impossible
and possibility.
O pellucid

medusa. O bijoux.
O gorgeous
misnomer.

Malaprops

Good writtens! Hailey writes,
submits her essay. *Done.*
A purple frowny face
concludes her thought.

My comp students mistake
loved ones for granite, write
with shame of kid complaints
about worn hammy-downs.

Hailey's final draft
approaches genre work:
a summer camp, a team
activity she knew

was stupid. Now she sees
some virtue in the game,
since "business majors need
teamwork." I write *Metaphor?*

Her girly postscript script
reads clearer than my own,
which should be twice as clear:
I have two hands; Hailey, none.

Nor ears. Nor legs to walk.
Her nose looks reconstructed.
Because she's trached, I lean
in close that time I hear

"house fire when I was five,"
butterfly tattoo alit
on countless girls not quite
aflutter on not-quite skin.

What did the artist think?
(I didn't lean in close
the time I heard her warn
a classmate "I will slap

you." Slap: "to hit someone
or something with the palm.")
In workshop, Hailey said
each camper's burns were "real

severe," though neither draft
acknowledges a fire
or aftermath, as if
I'd never seen the niche

a surgeon sculpted in
her wrist so she might grasp
a pen, though "grasp" perhaps
is not the best of words.

Beside her closing note
I ask my students write
I've written *Language, please.*
I don't believe in signs

like these—in faces sad
or happy—*which reduce*
our world to mimicry.
When I return their essays,

Hailey motors up
to me, paper pinched
between her stumps, and out
of courtesy I sit.

I look her in the eye.
She asks me what the hell
I wrote's supposed to say
then what the hell it means.

Crossing Guard at Acheron Elementary

Fuck your pinny, fuck your sign,
fuck your patently benign shamble
into stream of rush-hour traffic,
fuck your whistle-puckered lips,
cap, uniform so blue it's black,
fuck the nonchalance with which
you escort sleep-eyed, slap-happy
kids who sing *bo-bo ski wat-en*
tot-en kissy poo-poo leafy tree
from one side safely to the next,
fuck your engraved silver badge,
fuck the keenness of your gaze,
fuck finally, O Charon, the palm
you lift toward me to keep my mind
and engine idle as if I might divine
in it the fate of every passing child
which is—fuck me—my own.

Playboy's Guide to Lingering

We read *lingerie* as *lingering*.
An innocent mistake, yes, though

we didn't dally in Patel's humid
newsstand amid hanks of cigared

tobacco and men in coveralls logger-
heading with the Pennsylvania Lotto

to expand our budding tongues,
but to confuse the single shelf

of cryptograms and crosswords
with the candied shelves of pornos.

Despite our lousy decoding we proved
adept disrobers, kid-minds keen

to peel from skin what we'd later
call *satin* the way we peeled glossy

clementines slipped in our stockings,
our reward for a year of skirting Satan.

Nonchalant as bubble gum, we thumbed
them cover to cover, lingered, elbowed

one another, dittoed each sweet
image deep in memory's folds:

love's coy postures, saddle-stitched.
And that is how we imagined

it would be for us on those winter
afternoons: flimsy resistance, finger's

steady pressure, split of soft fruit.
We'd puzzle over language later.

For now, we had on our hands
more important things to misread.

Notes for the Next God

I want my god to hurt people.
I want my god the skylight
mid-shatter. I want my
god a grave-dropped aster.
I want my god the virus's
mutation. Glacier, flower:
debate the source of my god's
extinction. I want you ejected
through my god, to pick
from your face stray
shards of my god.
I want my god a glistening
diadem of offal. Turquoise
bruise. I want my god to deem
supplication the predeath
precrash high-speed lipstick
application. I want my god
in memoriam alleyway graffiti.
Quantify my god in light
pollution. I want my god
to fade spectacularly in empty
windows too high to touch.
I want my god to
batter your heart, deep-fry
your heart, serve your heart
to infidels on polystyrene.
Or the stranger's face she pictures
crushing, hot, atop her lover.
I want her lover to leave
in a caul of half-sleep

and search the twilit city
for an adulterated version
of my god.   I want my god
to turn her silk charmeuse
to worms.   I want my
god a malformed chamber
of the heart.   Chamber music
of the mind as it de-electrifies.
Echoed note as you
remember my god's here.
My god is in the chamber.

On Music

I like less and like it louder.
She likes it all but softer, daughter.
She doesn't dislike, she *prefers*.
I prefer the fast one softer.
I prefer the slow one louder.
Faster softer, slower louder.
Fast and soft for her is ether,
Own feet sounding time beneath her.
(Motion faster, volume lower.
She's the dizzy toddler spinner.)
I prefer my crooners louder,
Slower, numbers each year fewer.
I like less. Duende's rarer.
To disappear, I play them louder.
(I'm the older, further father
Cooking dinner.) *Turn it lower.*
I want louder, won't oblige her.
Set the timer. I've been harsher,
Slower, louder, faster, softer.

Last Request

We hitched the U-Haul trailer to his hearse.
Our friend was dead. Do this for me, he said,
then drive me through the town without remorse.

He claimed he heard a pastor chortle once
before a pious, piety-keen crowd
You'll never see a U-Haul on a hearse

and, henceforth, he refused to enter church.
Too smug. Each Sunday, quite alone, he prayed
then drove all over town to flee remorse.

This eased his guilt until the diagnosis.
What next? he thought. Recant? Rejoin the herd?
We hitched the U-Haul trailer to his hearse.

Unnerved by this postmortem vanitas,
we wept, as if grown suddenly afraid
we couldn't drive through town without remorse

until, that is, the pastor prayed *God bless
our friend, who both believed and unbelieved.*
We hitched the U-Haul trailer to his hearse,
then drove all over town without remorse.

Explication of Consciousness on a Day of Rain

In the rain of the mind a dimension exists
that is the increment between each thought,
a single mass of head-housed ambiance.
Its shape in the now is the shape of your life.

Resist that last point. The shape of your
life is each thought, not each unthought;
thus runs your counterargument as buses
bus nobody one block east and your attic

skylight frames rain as the ideal figure
for whatever you desire it to be this dawn.
Make small the universe for your own ends.
Make pockets for your unrequited hatreds.

Any erstwhile problem the mind adapts
to accommodate a newfound crisis.
Which in this gray conurbation is one
explication of consciousness on a day of rain.

Like you need explication. Like you'll
walk later in sunlight, kiss your daughter's
hair. Like small problems require small
solutions. Like you're ever really here.

Migration Theory

Some wiseacre claimed
   that birds migrate our heartland
      because they've grown too tired

to argue with the Sawtooths
   and Gallatins due west.
      My theory's wind, the way

wing cups the prairie air,
   cajoles that blood and bone
      to flight. So evenings we

drive south of town to watch
   the windmills—stems with three
      enormous blades aspin—

refuse more wild sky.
   Maybe one will take
      the wind's advice, I say,

and lift itself from earth.
   They aren't that wise, you say,
      a spare wing gets them nowhere.

The heart, you say, it loves
   the windmill's shape—the way
      it moves, the way it stays.

Entreaty

Crocuses, go away.

Purple shards purple the yard, shards of yellow yellow it.
Who tires not of such intrusive beauty?

Keep, I say, keep your anthers to yourselves. Your audacity.

As a child, I loved the wall whose copping was a mass
Of broken bottle glass: green, brown, blue

And only in the lowest sun illumined.

Surely atmosphere dulled each edge to gesture.
Any laceration required something broken

Broken again.

Manifesto

> *Art solves problems by making problems and makes problems by solving problems.*
>
> —Joseph J. Capista, "Manifesto"

Form: shape of the poem, shape of the chip
on your shoulder. Art doesn't need you.
It doesn't want to be your friend. Art wants
to annihilate you! Die-ins on the courthouse
stylobate beneath alabaster Lady Justice
areolae shimmering ketchuply in soft light
are, I think, political. I'm talking pure
star-dusty art that lays one hand gently
albeit firmly on your neck to still
your quavering head while the other depresses
the flusher. No, you needn't raise your hand
to go to the bathroom this is college.
Poems, as song, engage the temporal plane.
Speaking of the primacy of literary arts,
"font's" status as a Postclassical portmanteau
conjoining "form" and "content" is profound
poppycock—yes, I bet you pet one at the zoo,
"poppycock" being Middle Dutch for "soft
poop." Audacity/humility: poet's binary
brain lobes; poet: ever-dialectic virgule.
That Little Library book box beneath
the outsider art whirligig, i.e., mangled
farm implement which just last century
caused profound familial sorrow nay
tragedy given such soft and tiny fingers
and a bumper yield it's so easy to get ahead
of oneself in an age of rudimentary
technology and which was left to rust

until recontextualization via ennui
and spray paint—that little mausoleum
where anyone might take or leave with zilch
accountability a book of merit
by someone likely very dead—with what
a paltry axe I hew it down. Yes,
Deana, some of our greatest community
artists are practitioners of community arts,
thank you, De-*an*-a. What's my name?
Professor what? Prof. Sansabelt?
No grade's assigned to each poem draft
per se, which page eleven of the syllabus
articulates lucidly and in the most
immaculate of prose. It's a portfolio class.
Gestalt in the plastic arts is immediate:
we see the whole before we see each part.
Gestalt in the poem is retrospective:
we see each part before we see the whole.
Poems share the end of all art, to freeze
time, which they achieve by moving us
through time and this makes no sense.
Art's the failed negation of infinity.
Art comments on its very medium,
e.g., paintings on paint's capacity. So too
word, pastel, and yarn. Crocheting
vagina beer koozies sounds very empowering.
Did everybody hear that? Her—say your
name again—her art history professor said
Robert Motherwell said art's not an object
it's an experience. If I write *blue swimming
pool* you see a blue swimming pool and if
you write *blue swimming pool* I see a blue
swimming pool and we are thus ravished!
Well-behaved poems I find distasteful.
Anyone can write a brilliant poem. Once.

As for that epigraph, a cursory
internet search yields no exact matches
so while its sentiment remains passé
at least its syntax appears to be uniquely
my own. The poem's an investment
vehicle for social capital since, like, B.C.E.
I do not know whether you could have done
those cave paintings but you can't eat here
because this is a Smart Classroom and the kids
you nanny for, if I'm hearing you correctly,
their mom makes you pack a motivational
banana in their lunches which is a banana
with a motivational message written on it?
"We tame ink" is my bananagram of Ez.
Because I know it when I see it, I went to
a lot of school, speaker is persona is mask
as in trick-or-treat-this-is-a-stickup.
The mouse looks smaller when it's dead
until microbial proliferation begins
endeth a treatise on performance poetry.
*You think your rhymes historic / But they're
merely histrionic / You can't discern the
difference / If you ain't hooked on phonics.*
How's that? is what my driver's education
instructor used to say instead of saying Why?
Because we need at once to lose ourselves
and to cognize such loss, lest our lives be,
uh, bubbles not self-actualizing in the tar pit.
On didacticism: the teacher is a very good
enemy segues nicely into your bellyaching
yes you with the hickey about poems being
the one thing more gratuitous than manifestos.
Poetry is unnecessary. True too for mascara,
jacks, roman candles, well-nigh all commodities,
most everything we consume, pursue, desire.

"Jacks" is a game where you drop something
so you can then pick up another thing.
"If it is the highest wish of a man to live
undisturbed, he might be well advised to
remove art from his household." Wind, folks,
Edgar Wind. Art's the posing of a question.
The solitary answer: Death. You, the young,
resist and feel stirring in your soul those eternal
questions perhaps because you naïvely avow
you have a soul and probably none here shall
pursue the utmost of intimacies alone in a room
with a poem you never even realized you need
or need to write who cares you're young go
rock gondolas on the Ferris wheel go carouse
on your lit little carousels go flume à la log.
The Supreme Amusement Park's darkest
and most collapse-prone tunnel is always
love the line way too long and oh yes this
is the backside of a plastic hyperbolic swan
and with what an unrequited ache in our
rumps we persist my spouse and I have been
here since the moment we were tall enough
to ride this ride swans are actually very
aggressive creatures just do as they say so
nobody gets hurt a poem is anything that
demands a certain way of looking at nothing
and this deepness around us is dark hey guys
it's listening time not talking time, okay?
I think you might mean *domineering*
but I'll try to be less "diamond earing."
I'll try to stick that in a stupid poem.

Kid Happens

What things I love, I love
because they make no sense.
These riddles never solved
by logic's axe, for instance,

because they make no sense.
Oh, kids. We can't conceive
by logic's axe, for instance;
they happen and we praise,

Oh, kids! We can't conceive
these riddles never solved:
they happen and we praise.
What things I love, I love.

The American Crow and the Common Raven

Murder and unkindness, murder and unkindness.
As if we'd care to collect you, who collect anyway

on gnarled and barkless limbs with a mind to plague hawks.
Shit darker than a starling's, shit the color of bones.

Your bones are hollow. Whatever they once housed
must be the sheen on your plumes—just shadow

shellacked with black. We've asked you to stop
preaching at the funerals of strangers. You have not.

We've asked you to forget your perfect, lopsided
eggs. You have not. We can tax neither your broods

nor your beaks, full of obits and the silk of sweetcorn.
Cigars you pilfer from hats at the track are known

to burn barns. Hear? Barns have burned. Caw, cronk.
You shake your rag wings and out falls rainwater.

Death in Bitterroot Country

We buried you four fires deep.
Before I found you clutched in jagged
river ice, I searched lodgepoles

along the gulch, then spat, lit touchwood,
and dug through coals till the spade
split my boot sole, till a pick's handle

thickened my palms to coarser hide.
Only those easily dead, you said,
lie in easy graves. Then you left.

I picture you walking the river's frozen
throat for miles. It does not swallow you
the way, spring, it swallowed a child.

I try not to admire the nine cold
moons left by your nails where you,
for whatever reason, nearly climbed out.

When I kissed your rose-starved lips,
the elders uttered their logging camp oaths,
wasps abuzz in wise hives of their lives.

No one mentioned your cries beside
the Boiling River, its name still heavy
and particulate silt inside my gut.

Wife, this poultice on my chest is grief:
a drowned daughter's hair, ash, soft bud cut
from your tongue, sweetgrass, bitterroot.

Don't tell me what I've failed to do.
With you gone, I forgot my mouth tasting
like a stranger's loose teeth. Forgot you

shattered blue china, gathered it in your shoes,
then scattered it, barefoot, along the shoals
for her, you said, for her to follow home.

The Lovers

After Magritte's Les Amants, 1928

Our end starts here:
    tonight we wish
upon the darkest
    star, entwine
as beasts, lament our
    breath's capacity
to take and give
    small secrets
we offer this world
    only when its
back is turned.
    Be crush, love.
Be lush. Undoing,
    undone. Be sunset.
I'll be the blackest
    sails ever raised
against you, perfumed
    by empires fallen.
And when I die, if I
    die wise, you will
know I have lived
    as a fool.

Composition

What I like about my students is that they aren't yet the sum
of their worst actions, that they define themselves
not by what they've done but by what they'll do.
Each is a primer on orientation. None will last for long.

In middle age it's hard to know what one has done
and one has failed to do, especially come spring
when the world won't cease its own undoing and thus
obscures profoundly one's measure of oneself.

Alone beneath the attic skylight, I convince myself
I'm looking at a world and not this sky I watch change
before my eyes: first cloud, then bird, then dappled star.
Some iridescent falling satellite. I close my eyes

And it is gone. *Blue*, I write beneath the skylight, *eternal
understudy for eternity*. Too stilted to be of any use,
this line's supposed to foreground our need to conceive
limitations no matter their futility, e.g., the way blue

Might stand for both heaven's periphery as well as,
impossibly, for heaven itself. We expect lines to behave
this way, be they in a poem or a drawing. This reminds
me of something I read once in *The Presentation of Self*

In Everyday Life, a college text whose margins I annotated
with a vim possible only for one who understands
nothing of what he has read, for whom the text is a line
between the self and the world and not the world itself.

When my roommate's father drove into a tree that spring
	because he could no longer bear his wife's diagnosis,
	everybody understood what we refused to believe:
	that this was his final line of argument with a world.

Now both are dead, husband and wife. Because I've lost
	touch with my college roommate I do not know how
	he has learned to love the world, whether he is
	terrified by those in whose arms he lies or whether

He terrifies them with a violence he did not choose.
	Printed on the underside of this poem draft I reread
	now is a rubric I composed to assess my students'
	epiphantic essays. I focus on the poem's lines,

But it's impossible to not notice language bleeding through
	the paper in reverse, so I flip the page to read my words.
	"Wonder" is archaic, says the longhand student note I
	wrote before I placed this sheet in the reuse bin because

In haste I miswrote *"Yonder."* I read my typed criteria:
	Essay articulates author's change in worldview,
	Prose reads clean and precise, rows of boxes labeled
	Good, Fair, Poor. My big grown-up epiphany, I told

My roommate, is that for so many others the interior life
	is of no consequence and they are profoundly happy.
	He had not yet had any big grown-up epiphanies,
	he said. My students often say the same and protest

This assignment which, they also say, I should not grade
	because it's totally personal. Objectivity's their religion.
	They want truth neat and fair. Me too. In the essay I
	keep writing in my head, I hold each daughter's hand.
Petals fall as we sing silly songs. *Cherry blossoms fall*

like rain, I write, staccato drops darkening the skylight.
Or, *I wished that cherry blossoms fell on us like rain.*
Or, *I wish cherry blossoms fell on us instead of rain.*

It's here that I keep getting stuck, halfway between
    wonder and distance while I recall a puddle filled
    with rain and blossoms, an edge measured in petals.
    One fell on us. This mattered to me more than anything.

As If the Lullaby Is for the Child

O babychild
            Listen
      This is all
   I know:
      When for *Twinkle*,
         Twinkle   I sing
            Tyger, Tyger
                  The melody
                        Still holds.

Notes and Acknowledgments

"Thaw": This poem borrows "unquiet dreams" from W. B. Yeats's "The Stolen Child."

"The Beautiful Things of the Earth Become More Dear as They Elude Pursuit": This poem borrows its title from Thomas Hardy's *Desperate Remedies*. Gratitude to Daniel Anderson.

"40": This poem references Brian Eno's 1975 album *Another Green World*.

"Guide to the Monumental City": This poem's title owes a debt to Cindy Kelly's *Outdoor Sculpture in Baltimore: A Historical Guide to Public Art in the Monumental City*.

"Devotional of Daily Apprehension": This poem is dedicated to my teacher, the late poet and critic Daniel McGuiness.

"In the Event of a Fire," "Gut-Bomb," "Johnny Salmon's Father Enters the Shelter Unannounced to Repo His Adjudicated Son," and "Vigilante Day Parade" are for my former charges at the Margaret Stuart Shelter and the Jan Shaw Youth Home.

"Malaprops" is for J.M.

"On Music" is for Moira.

"As If the Lullaby Is for the Child" is for Aoife.

Thanks to the editors of the journals in which these poems appeared, sometimes in a different form:

AGNI: "Kid Happens," "Telescope"
America: "In the Event of a Fire"
Beloit Poetry Journal: "SOWEBO"

Cimarron Review: "Faces of Death"

The Cincinnati Review: "Crossing Guard at Acheron Elementary"

Colorado Review: "History of the Inevitable"

CutBank: "Notes for the Next God"

The Georgia Review: "Cornicello"

The Hopkins Review: "On Music"

The Hudson Review: "The Beautiful Things of the Earth Become More Dear as They Elude Pursuit," "Explication of Consciousness on a Day of Rain"

Image: "Entreaty" ("Having seen"), "Mid-Flight, Mid-Ascension Virgin Photograph"

Innisfree Poetry Journal: "The Lovers"

The Journal: "Jellyfish"

JuJubes: "Vigilante Day Parade"

Literary Imagination: "Exit Wound"

Little Patuxent Review: "For a Daughter"

Measure: "Malaprops," "Thaw"

North American Review: "Death in Bitterroot Country"

Ploughshares: "Gut-Bomb"

Poetry Northwest: "40"

Quarterly West: "The American Crow and the Common Raven"

Slate: "Playboy's Guide to Lingering"

Smartish Pace: "Last Request," "Thirtysomething Blues"

Sow's Ear Poetry Review: "A Child Bird-Scarer"

Texas Observer: "Johnny Salmon's Father Enters the Shelter Unannounced to Repo His Adjudicated Son," "Migration Theory"

Valparaiso Poetry Review: "Lost Children"

"Telescope" was also published online by *Poetry Daily*.

Thanks to the astonishing community that is the Warren Wilson College MFA Program for Writers, especially to Debra Allbery, Rodney Jones, Mary Leader, James Longenbach, Heather McHugh, Alan Shapiro, and Ellen Bryant Voigt. Thanks, too, to the Warren Wilson College MFA Academic Board. To all the writers at Loyola University Maryland, Iowa State University, and The West Chester University Poetry Conference: thank you. The Bread Loaf Writers' Conference and the Sewanee Writers' Conference offered their support in the completion of these poems, as did the National Endowment for the Humanities, the Maryland State Arts Council, and Towson University's College of Liberal Arts and Department of English. Thank you, Neal Bowers, Lara Egger, Karen Fish,

Daisy Fried, Naomi Shihab Nye, Matthew Westbrook, and all the good folks at Beveridge & Diamond. Profound and enduring gratitude to Beth Ann Fennelly for selecting this book for the Hollis Summers Poetry Prize, as well as to David Sanders and Ohio University Press.

Abundant thanks to Joe and Anne Capista and to James and Anne Curran, whose enduring support and generosity has made possible many things, including the writing of these poems. Thank you, Moira. Thank you, Aoife. Thank you, finally, Shannon Curran for patience, faith, and love: *I do, I will, I am.*